The Language
of Roses

AvTrechslin.

STELVIO COGGIATTI

The Language
of Roses

Color plates by
ANNE MARIE TRECHSLIN

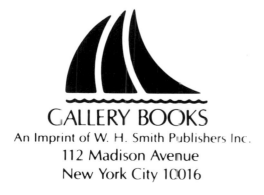

GALLERY BOOKS
An Imprint of W. H. Smith Publishers Inc.
112 Madison Avenue
New York City 10016

Published by Gallery Books
A Division of W.H. Smith Publishers, Inc.
112 Madison Avenue
New York, New York 10016

Translated by Mary Fitton

Printed and bound in Italy by
Arnoldo Mondadori Editore, Verona

Contents

Preface

I love all flowers, roses most of all, and I do my best to understand their needs, but the concept of a language of roses made me stop and think. People who claim they talk to flowers rarely tell us in what tongue their colloquies take place but nobody, I imagine, will dispute that roses speak to us through their beauty; and so our dialogue with them is well begun with the faithful and detailed portraits in these pages.

Beauty is not the only means of communication, however. The gamut of expression belonging to this language is infinitely richer than this alone, encompassing many different devices and associations. Does the rose, for instance, try to charm us with its fragrance, or is scent merely a part of its native elegance? And consider the contrast in effect between the straight stem of some opulent 1850s bloom and the pliant stalks of a tea-scented rose, matching the modish langour of fin de siècle ladies. Both roses are similar in a way, because created by a single master, yet different in a thousand delicate details and in the visual message they convey.

Every rose in this book inspires the conversation, as it were, instructing us as to botanical or popular names, membership of a particular family or group, habit, vigour, resistance to cold and disease and suitability for growing in the open. Our dialogue with roses should include listening to them, so as to recognize their vital need for food and water, pruning and pesticides. It is a difficult art, this listening, but we must attend, divine the message, and do as they bid us.

Stelvio Coggiatti

The Roses

Rosa damascena semperflorens

Rosa damascena semperflorens (known in the Roman era); syn. *Rosa damascena bifera.*

Although evidence is lacking, it is generally believed that this rose originated in a natural cross between *Rosa gallica*, the wild species of Europe and the Near East, and *Rosa moschata*, which hails from the same regions and flowers from August to October. We know that the Romans had only one remontant, or repeat-flowering, rose (the Latin word *biferum* means "twice bearing"), and cytologic tests point to a very ancient ancestry for *Rosa damascena semperflorens*.

Pierre Joseph Redouté (1759–1840) the French flower painter who always gave rose names in French and Latin, labels one of his watercolours *Rosa damascena italica – La quatre-saisons d'Italie*. This Italian attribution must derive from the belief that the damask rose had grown in Paestum, where rose gardens flowered twice a year – *canerem biferique rosaria Paesti*, says Virgil in *The Georgics* – while the blooms of September, October and November, following the usual flush in late April, would suggest the optimistic *quatre-saisons*.

The Jesuit botanist, Father G.B. Ferrari, mentions a "perpetual-flowering Italian rose" in his Latin edition of *Flora, seu de Florum cultura* (1633) and again in the Italian edition of 1638, where it is a *rosa italiana d'ogni mese*. He describes its colour as a soft red but we have to assume that despite his otherwise excellent reputation he must have accepted faulty oral evidence for this claim without checking, for a true red untinged with purple was unknown until China roses were introduced into the West. Father Ferrari may, however, have been referring to a stray *Rosa chinensis semperflorens*, three centuries before the generally agreed date of its first appearance in Europe.

Rosa canina

Rosa canina (known in the Roman period); syn. *Rosa canina* 'Pollmeriana.'

In Book xxv of *Naturalis Historia* Pliny the Elder discusses the widespread faith in a decoction of the root of *cynorrhodon* – the *Rosa canina* of Linnaeus – as remedy for the bite of a rabid dog, and illustrates with an anecdote the contemporary faith of learned and simple alike in this vain cure. The trust is enshrined in the rose's botanical name.

With its glossy leaves and pale petals, the variety of *Rosa canina* shown here – selected and distributed by Herr Pollmer, of Grossenhain in Germany – is perhaps the most attractive. It is one of the few roses used by breeders all over the world in their search for the ideal stock on which to graft the perfect garden rose or cut flower. *Rosa canina* 'Pollmeriana' is very vigorous, resistant to drought and cold and, though it is not happy in sea air and has a short grafting period (confined to the beginning of the season), it will give splendid results with roses intended for the greenhouse. Its fruits are regarded as an important source of Vitamin C.

Rosa alba semiplena

Rosa alba semiplena (possibly known in the Roman period); syn. *R. alba suaveolens*.

The German botanist Hermann Christ suggested in *Die Rosen der Schweiz* (1873) that this species is a hybrid; later research by Dr C.C. Hurst leads us to suppose that *R. alba* almost certainly derives from some natural pollination of *R. canina froebelii* by *R. damascena* (itself a hybrid of *R. gallica* and *R. moschata*).

To define the prototypical shape and form of *Rosa alba* is practically impossible, though the principal varieties – *R. alba incarnata* (syn. 'Cuisse de Nymphe'), *Alba maxima* and *Alba semiplena* – are recognized as corresponding to descriptions in ancient writers. According to W. J. Bean's *Trees and Shrubs Hardy in the British Isles, incarnata* differs from the white rose in the number of leaflets, a more or less complete absence of prickles, and in the pale blush pink of the petals. It is also known that *R. alba maxima* and *R. alba semiplena* are each a mutation of the other, as is proved by clear and frequent cases of reversion. In the species and varieties alike the petals tend to lie flat, and the highly scented flowers are of irregular shape.

At Kazanlik, the famous Bulgarian Valley of Roses, the essential oil extracted for perfume comes mainly from petals of *R. damascena trigintipetala*, and only a small proportion from the sweetly scented *Rosa alba*.

14

Rosa glauca

Rosa glauca (1788); syn. *R. rubrifolia* (1789), *R. rubicunda* (1797), *R. ferruginea* (name not officially recognized).

The great attraction of this species lies not in the small flowers, which are single and short-lived, but in the delicate and unusual leaf colouring. Graham Stuart Thomas, a sharp observer, noted the grey-blue bloom on the leaves from spring to autumn, how the leaf blade broadens out, assuming tones of lilac-grey in cool, shady situations, and how it shrinks in full sun, taking on a tint of coppery violet. The effect of this almost entirely thornless rose, with its little clusters of unostentatious single flowers and young stems of a pronounced violet colour, is one of lightness and charm. The sprays, even without blossom, will lend elegance to imaginative flower arrangements all year round.

Vigorous specimens are best obtained from seed or cuttings rather than by grafting, for unless there has been chance or deliberate cross-pollination, the seedlings of species roses will always breed true. Much of this plant's reputation rests on simplicity of line and delicacy of colour. Its classification, however, has been unclear. In 20 years botanists have given it four different names, the most popular and generally used of which *R. rubrifolia*, has now been demoted to a synonym and replaced by *R. glauca*. Although the term *rubrifolia* is found in a description written in 1789, *glauca* had appeared in another the year before, and, under Article 63 of the International Code of Botanical Nomenclature, the earlier name must prevail.

Rosa chinensis pallida

Rosa chinensis pallida (1752); syn. 'Old Blush,' 'Common Blush.'

The ancestral species named *Rosa chinensis* by Jacquin of Leyden in 1768 is probably extinct, and the name is now applied to the garden roses of Chinese origin descended from it. To begin with, specimens were very scarce and designations, as a result, confused; names such as *Rosa indica* and *Rosa bengalensis*, were changed when found to be geographically incorrect.

Between the end of the eighteenth century and the beginning of the nineteenth, Chinese roses, including the example illustrated here, introduced into Europe the much desired characteristic of remontancy – the ability to flower again from late summer to autumn. According to experts such as Willmott, Bean and Young, *R. chinensis pallida*, though of uncertain parentage, may have resulted from a distant chance pollination of the original species more than a thousand years ago. Its appearance in ancient Chinese textile patterns seems to confirm this theory.

In eighteenth-century England popular names for the newly arrived China roses would emphasize some special quality. 'Blush,' for instance, evoked the pale pink colour, and the 'Monthly Rose' would flower throughout the year.

Rosa chinensis pallida may have contributed more than any other rose to the modern hybrids and was certainly the first to provide new strains in America, Africa and Europe through proven crossings with the following:

– *Rosa damascena semperflorens*, most likely by random natural fertilization in the island of Réunion, off the African coast, near Mauritius. Réunion, then a French colony, was known as the Ile de Bourbon, and this crossing gave rise to the Bourbon roses.

– *Rosa moschata*, the result of manual pollination effected by John Champneys, a rice planter in Charleston. The Noisette brothers, one of whom lived in Charleston, the other in Paris, marketed the seedlings on both sides of the Atlantic and Noisette roses later contributed to the Hybrid Teas.

Further crossings with Bourbon roses and with other descendants of the China roses led to the Hybrid Perpetuals, which were to be absorbed in the Hybrid Teas.

AMTrechslin.

Rose de Meaux

'Rose de Meaux' (c. 1800); syn. *Rosa centifolia* 'Pomponia.'

Three great rose painters have made watercolour portraits of this small, though not miniature rose: Pierre-Joseph Redouté, whose 'Rose Pomponia' is plate 65 in vol. I of *Les Roses*; Alfred Parsons, who gives it the same name in plate 119, vol. II of Ellen Willmott's *The Genus Rosa*; and, in this book, Anne Marie Trechslin. Spanning nearly 200 years, from 1816 to 1986, these pictures show how the deepening of colour from the pale outer petals towards the center has remained a constant characteristic throughout that time.

Names such as *R. burgundensis* and *R. burgundica*, which should obviously belong to the Pompon *R. centifolia* 'Parvifolia,' have been attached to the 'Rose de Meaux,' and doubts as to its kinship with *Rosa centifolia* may well arise from the confusion in classification thus created between roses of diverse shape and form.

Ellen Willmott puts forward the reasonable theory that the name commemorates bishop Doménique Seguier, predecessor of Bossuet, the Eagle of Meaux. A keen gardener, Seguier grew 18 types of rose with considerable skill, and the combination of spiritual and botanical interests must have made him a figure of mark in his cathedral town.

Finally we may note that the Flemish painters preferred *Rosa centifolia* above any other rose, and that what we call *Rosa centifolia* is quite unrelated to the flower so designated in ancient Rome. The name, unused for more than 1,000 years, was revived in seventeenth-century Holland, to be adopted and endorsed by Linnaeus in the eighteenth century for a very double, pale pink scented rose of globular form.

Rosa centifolia cristata

Rosa centifolia cristata (1829); syn. 'Chapeau de Napoléon,' 'Crested Moss.'

To the French this variety, discovered by an unknown gardener in Switzerland soon after their former Emperor's death, was 'Chapeau de Napoléon' because of the unusual shape of the buds, each one surrounded by a "cockade" of sepals. The English were not to be outdone in the coining of popular names, although in correctly translating *cristata* as "crested" they confused the issue by adding the word "moss." A true Moss Rose is one descended from *Rosa centifolia*, having the typical "moss" or lacy, glandular covering on calyx, peduncle and sepals, and only when this is present can a rose be so classed. (There can be confusion with the botanical species *Rosa moschata*, whose scent is said to resemble animal musk, particularly that secreted by the glands of Moschus moschiferus, the Asian hornless deer.)

The variety shown here is a *centifolia*, though it would be interesting to know the origin of the thickly "crested" outline of the sepals, to which the buds owe their characteristic shape. One theory suggests a random mutation (though not that which gave rise to the future Moss Roses), while Roy E. Shepherd, author of *History of the Rose*, believes that the typical crests were first displayed by a seedling of *Rosa centifolia*.

The earliest description of *Rosa centifolia cristata*, which dates from 1829, denies any connection between the swelling of the buds and the soft, fragrant coating of the Moss Roses; modern rosarians such as Paul, Parsons, Bunyard, Hurst and Thomas have agreed on this point. Yet seven years later, when William Curtis, editor of the famous *Botanical Magazine* (the only botanical journal published continuously from 1787 to the present day), offered his readers the first, modest coloured drawing of this rose, he rekindled the controversy. The accompanying notes were headed "Rosa centifolia, muscosa; cristata. Crested var. of the Moss Rose," and, in praising the beauty of the flowers, included the words, "independently of the curious mode in which the moss springs in tufts from the edges of its calyx."

AmTrechslin·

Gloire de Dijon

'Gloire de Dijon' (1853).

Samuel Reynolds Hole, Dean of Rochester, the first and much esteemed President of the National Rose Society, holding office from 1877 to 1904, was author of *A Book about Roses*, a popular title on the subject (26 editions appeared between 1869 and 1910). In Chapter VIII Dean Hole writes: "I lose no time in stating that the best climbing Rose with which I am acquainted is that which has just announced itself, Gloire de Dijon, commonly classed with the tea-scented China roses, but more closely resembling the Noisette family in its robust growth and hardy constitution. (...) If ever, for some heinous crime, I were miserably sentenced, for the rest of my life, to possess but a single rose-tree, I should desire to be supplied, on leaving the dock, with a strong plant of Gloire de Dijon."

With all its merits, however, this rose is not perhaps a good developer of fine examples. Under the most favourable conditions the shoots will climb to a height of six meters and, unless fan-trained, develop no basal foliage. Both Jack Harkness and the late Patrick M. Synge note a risk of diminished vigour in clones of 'Gloire de Dijon' – that is, groups of roses bred by agamic, or asexual, propagation from the original seedling.

Rosa banksiae lutescens

Rosa banksiae lutescens (introduced into Europe, 1870).

This *Rosa banksiae* – named after the wife of Sir Joseph Banks, the naturalist who sailed with Captain Cook – is yellow (as the word *lutescens* implies) and scented, with clusters of small, five-petalled flowers.

It hails from China, where grave difficulties beset the English traveller in the early decades of the nineteenth century and "plant hunters" might botanize only in the immediate surroundings of the larger cities. By way of compensation, however, the garden and nursery plants raised for their decorative value usually proved more attractive than those found in the wild. They were often scented, and the flowers could be spectacular.

The first two specimens of *R. banksiae* seen in the United Kingdom were double-flowered. One, introduced in 1807, was white with a perfume reminiscent of violets; the other, an almost unscented yellow, was welcomed all the same as being less susceptible to frost.

Ellen Willmott, in *The Genus Rose*, mentions a *Rosa banksiae* that had grown in the grounds of a Scottish castle since the end of the eighteenth century. It had never flowered, she says, until transferred to a garden on the Côte d'Azur where, in 1909, it produced white blossoms, single and perfumed. This, clearly, was the original botanical species. Yet in 1877 the Bulletin of the *Società Toscana di Orticultura* (The Horticultural Society of Tuscany) records that Paolo Baroni, head gardener at the Orto Botanico in Florence, had successfully gathered a few seeds from the scanty stamens and anthers of a bush of *R.b.* 'Alba plena' and from them raised three plants, two white, one yellow and all of them, unlike the parent, single-flowered.

We know from contemporary sources that *R.b. lutescens* was brought to England by Sir Thomas Hanbury in 1871 from his recently created garden at La Mortola, near Ventimiglia on the Riviera. And if it seems surprising that a Chinese rose should have originated in Italy, we should remember the Hanbury family's close contacts with China. Sir Thomas had developed a flourishing business as well as fulfilling consular duties in that country.

It is interesting to note that these roses – the first single-flowered *banksiae*, bred by Baroni, and Hanbury's *lutescens* – both began their Western careers in Italy. We can only assume that to grow in Europe they required the mild Mediterranean climate.

Mme Alfred Carrière

'Mme Alfred Carrière' (1879).

Lyons, birthplace of Joseph Schwartz who raised 'Mme Alfred Carrière,' produced many fine nurserymen and plant breeders during the last century. Schwartz was responsible for other marvellous roses, including 'La Tosca,' 'Mme Ernest Calvat,' 'La Reine Victoria' and 'Roger Lambelin,' which have played an important part in modern rose breeding. Schwartz's business continued after his death, thanks to its established reputation, to seedlings still under test and to the managerial skills of his widow who, if we may trust the *Nomenclature de tous les noms des roses* (Paris, 1906), herself discovered 57 new roses. Schwartz discovered 63.

There is some doubt over the customary classification of 'Mme Alfred Carrière' as a Noisette rose, for its parentage is unknown and objective examination reveals the globular corolla of the Bourbon varieties, and characteristics, including the scent, which suggest the Tea Roses. But it remains, nevertheless, a valued and popular climber, sound, vigorous and remontant.

Mrs John Laing

'Mrs John Laing' (1887).

This is one of the repeat-flowering roses called by the French *Hybrides remontants* and by the English – a touch too hopefully, perhaps – Hybrid Perpetuals, which originated in the early part of the last century in the crossing of *Rosa damascena semperflorens* with European descendants of *Rosa chinensis*.

Graham Stuart Thomas dislikes these remontant hybrids because for a time they displaced the old shrub roses whose leading and most learned champion he is. But now, as he says, "The hordes of Hybrid Perpetuals have gone, except for a handful of tried favourites." He heads the very short list with 'Mrs John Laing.'

In the late nineteenth century a raiser of hybrid cattle named Henry Bennett first applied the techniques of stock-breeding in his deliberately planned crossing and selective propagation of roses. There was horrified criticism from outraged rosarians, but his ideas were vindicated with a gold medal for 'Her Majesty,' and another for 'Mrs John Laing,' from what was then the National Rose Society. (The "Royal" was added in 1965.) As always in those days, the awards were offered for cut flowers; it was not until 1929, in the face of some prejudice and hostility, that the United Kingdom had any competitions, such as are widespread today, for bushes grown under test conditions.

The Revd A. Foster-Melliar, author of *The Book of the Rose* (1905) considered 'Mrs John Laing' to be a rose for everyone, the rose with the fewest drawbacks. Among its virtues he cites its excellent value in the garden (he was writing, we should remember, at a time when flowering was not continual as it is now), its resistance to mildew, the number of petals, the flower-form and strong scent. Nowadays, 'Mrs John Laing' is rated 8.2 out of 10 in the American Rose Society's *Handbook for Selecting Roses*.

Rosa sericea pteracantha

Rosa sericea pteracantha (introduced into Europe from China, 1890); syn. *R. omoiensis pteracantha*.

There are those who think the thorns of a plant are for defense; others, to help it cling and climb; and some, including the French writer and keen gardener Alphonse Karr (1808–90), regard thorns as the necessary price to pay for the ultimate reward, the flower.

> *De leur meilleur côté*
> *Tâchons de voir les choses.*
> *Vous vous plaignez de voir*
> *Les rosiers épineux*
> *Et je rend grâce aux dieux*
> *Que les épines aient des roses!*

> (Oh, why lament the thorny ring
>   Which girds the roses round?
> Far better you rejoice, and sing,
>   That with those thorns are roses found!)

And the rose without a thorn is by no means unknown, whatever the proverb says. 'Smooth Velvet,' 'Smooth Lady' and 'Smooth Angel' are three completely thornless new varieties put on the market by a Californian breeder in 1986.

But even the greatest devotee of the smooth stem must admire the defensive thorns, huge and handsome and unlike any others, on the young growth of *Rosa sericea pteracantha*. These red, transparent daggers catch the eye immediately, before it is attracted to the flowers, though they, too, can claim an interesting distinction. In the whole genus *Rosa*, these are the only four-petalled single flowers; all the rest, save those of *Rosa sericea* and its varieties, have five petals.

The word *pteracantha*, derived from the Greek *pteròn*, a wing, and *acantha*, thorn, emphasizes the "winged" shape of the thorns.

Mme Caroline Testout

'Mme Caroline Testout' (1890).

This variety is still to be seen in many gardens. A long-lived rose, it is widely admired for its prolific bearing of several blooms to a stem, for its repeat-flowering, luminous pink colour, intense perfume and the globular flower shape, resulting from the large number of petals. It is also easily propagated from autumn cuttings.

The lady who gave her name to this rose, Caroline Testout, was a very fashionable French *modiste*. Planning to open a London branch of her business, she decided that what she required was a trademark – and opted for a rose whose elegance, scent and colour would be linked with her name. She persuaded Joseph Pernet-Ducher, "the wizard of Lyons," to let her have full rights in one of his new roses, to be called 'Caroline Testout.'

Since the early years of the twentieth century 'Mme Caroline Testout' has been the reigning star in the parks, gardens and streets of Portland, Oregon. The National Rose Society's Annual for 1916 reported that the municipal authorities there had planted an incredible three million bushes.

Fimbriata

'Fimbriata' (1891).

The rose, as undisputed queen of all flowers, need never imitate one of her subjects; yet some descendants of crosses between *Rosa rugosa* and varieties of *Rosa multiflora* and *Rosa noisettiana* (now merged with the Hybrid Teas) with their short, pronouncedly fringed, or "fimbriate," petals give their flowers the appearance of carnations. These so called carnation-roses are more or less restricted to four main types, though others may be unrecorded:

– The oldest, 'Fimbriata' or 'Dianthiflora,' is the attested offspring of *Rosa rugosa*, the pollinator having been 'Mme Alfred Carrière.' Few of the qualities of that white climber are, however, evident in 'Fimbriata,' which is bushy, with crinkly leaves and scented pink petals, and which needs high humidity and fertile soil.

– 'F. J. Grootendorst' (*Rosa rugosa rubra* x 'Mme Norbert Levavasseur,' a red polyantha, 1918) is remontant, with small unscented flowers borne abundantly in thick clusters.

– 'Pink Grootendorst,' 1923. This is a sport from the last-named variety and has similar qualities, save that it is bright pink and less vigorous.

– 'Grootendorst Supreme,' 1936. Another mutant from 'F.J. Grootendorst,' this rose lacks stamina and is less popular than 'Pink Grootendorst,' having even smaller flowers, though of a fine dark red.

The name Grootendorst is that of the firm of breeders at Boskoop in Holland which introduced these three varieties.

A.M.TRECHSLIN.

Blanc Double de Coubert

'Blanc Double de Coubert' (1892).

The purest white of all white roses, disease-free, extremely resistant to frost, tolerates sandy soil and coastal winds, and retains its scent after nightfall – what sounds like a list of unheard of perfections is an accurate enumeration of the qualities of 'Blanc Double de Coubert.' However, we might add in all honesty that too alkaline a soil will not suit it, and that it makes no growth in the first year after planting, but these are minor blemishes.

The array of virtues is shared by many other descendants of the Sino-Japanese *Rosa rugosa*, a species conventionally faulted as having flowers unsuitable for decorative arrangements. But the semi-double blooms bred from it will live for nearly a week indoors if cut just as they are opening, and may be forgiven for lacking extravagantly long stems.

Outdoors, 'Blanc Double de Coubert' will successfully furnish the bare stem of a grafted standard rose, filling the space with its deeply wrinkled (*rugosa*) foliage, while the flowers – an extra advantage – harmonize with any colour.

This rose was bred by the famous rosarian Cochet-Cochet at Coubert in the Seine-et-Marne, and the words *blanc* and *double* remind us that the white petals of the variety are more plentiful than those of the species.

Baron Girod de l'Ain

'Baron Girod de l'Ain' (1897).

One of the last of the Hybrid Perpetuals, this rose was soon popular and widely grown. It is still to be met with today, though these hybrids, dominant for more than 50 years over the Pernetiana and Noisette roses later incorporated with the Hybrid Teas, and over the tea-scented roses unsuitable for harsh climates, seemed out of favour by the end of the nineteenth century. But over 3,000 varieties of them were known in Europe, half of which are flourishing at the Roseraie de l'Haÿ near Paris.

The descent of the Hybrid Perpetuals long as it is, may be summarized thus:

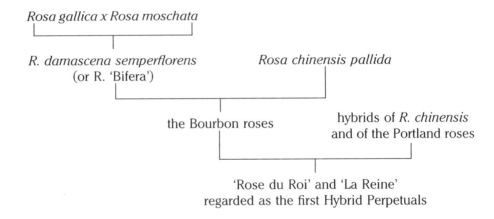

Rosa gallica x Rosa moschata

R. damascena semperflorens (or R. 'Bifera')

Rosa chinensis pallida

the Bourbon roses

hybrids of *R. chinensis* and of the Portland roses

'Rose du Roi' and 'La Reine' regarded as the first Hybrid Perpetuals

'Baron Girod de l'Ain' is a sport, originating not from seed but as a mutant growth. A mutant, though genetically very complex, is explained in simple terms as an anomalous growth produced from a bud on a rosebush and differing markedly from the parent plant. The difference may be in some organic function (in being thornless, for example, or scented, or of a new colour or possessing twice as many petals); in habit (climbing, perhaps, instead of bushy); or in its qualities, such as remontancy where the original flowers only once a year. When the new characteristics are judged worth preserving the attempt to 'fix' them is made by test-growing specimens taken from the branches on which the mutant first occurred.

'Baron Girod de l'Ain' first occurred on a double-flowered rose named 'Eugène Fürst,' equally scented and remontant, but without the white edging seen on the petals of the mutant. Of the few roses with this edging – 'Pride of Reigate' and 'Roger Lamelin' among them – 'Baron Girod de l'Ain' is considered the most beautiful.

AMTRECHSLIN.

Dorothy Perkins

'Dorothy Perkins' (1901).

When in 1908 a referendum was held among members of the National Rose Society to find out what were the favourite climbers and to establish a grading, it was discovered that, in the "cluster-flowered" class, 63% of the votes went to a rose introduced seven years previously by Jackson and Perkins (then of Newark, New Jersey): 'Dorothy Perkins,' a descendant of *Rosa wichuraiana.*

The wealth of its double flowers will form a thick pink canopy of readily trained sprays above a terrace, or luxuriate on a wide pergola, or even cascade in a graceful weeping willow shape over a wild briar understock.

'Dorothy Perkins' flowers late, long and abundantly, so that its lack of repeat-flowering, scentlessness and tendency to mildew hardly matter. Easy to cultivate and to increase from cuttings, it reigned supreme, with its red-flowered twin, 'Excelsa,' into the 1940s and 50s, but as time went on and other roses, remontant, scented and resistant to mildew, became available, the defects were more noticeable. For all that, A.H. Williams, acknowledged expert on wichuraianas, was probably right when, speaking of their fall from favour, he claimed that they "would be more highly praised were they not so ridiculously easy to grow."

Belle Portugaise

'Belle Portugaise' (1903).

Seldom can the Royal Horticultural Society's prestigious Award of Merit have gone to a rose introduced 56 years before, but 'Belle Portugaise,' a rose of 1903, won it when shown by G.S. Thomas, then Director of the Sunningdale Nurseries in Surrey, on 15th May, 1959. Though late, the recognition was well deserved. For one thing, it showed that this lovely rose, given a sunny situation and shelter from cold winds, will succeed elsewhere than on the French and Italian rivieras and in similar surroundings usually thought suitable for it. In his book on climbers G.S. Thomas cites a fine old plant of this vigorous rose covering a wall in the Royal Horticultural Society gardens at Wisley in Surrey.

The remarkable vigour of this rose is apparently inherited in the first place from its seed parent *Rosa gigantea* (the Wild Tea Rose), as well as from the pollinator, the climber 'Reine Marie Henriette.' The breeder, Henri Cayeux, was French, and Director of the Estufa Fria, or municipal hothouse gardens, at Lisbon.

Rosa multiflora cathayensis

Rosa multiflora cathayensis (introduced into the West, 1907).

This variety of the species *Rosa multiflora* originates in China, or, as Marco Polo called that land, Cathay. Botanically it belongs to the section known as the Synstylae (from the Greek *syn*, "together with" and *stylos*, "pistil") which is characterized by the pistil formed of fused, protruding styles, flat flower-clusters, profuse and scented flowers, and climbing or bushy growth. Of these features the first, the combination of several pistils into what is seen as a single column, is specific, the others being also found in plants of other sections.

This is a very vigorous rose, putting out numerous climbing branches every year, and capable of reaching a height of 6 meters if supported. Resembling the species in its rich late-spring flowering and a winter-long abundance of small, round fruits in orange-red clusters, it surpasses it in the beauty of the arching sprays and the size and colour of the flowers, which are pale pink, five-petalled like those of *R. multiflora*, but larger. Their grace is rivalled by the almost geometrical perfection of the regular corymbs, whose secondary stems carry from five to seven flowers each. The greenish fused pistil, surrounded by a great number of bright yellow stamens, is extremely prominent. The leaves, of a beautiful opaque green in fine contrast with the light green stems, consist of five to seven oval-lanceolate leaflets, rather rough, like blackberry leaves, their undersides downy and grey-blue.

Though not remontant, this rose is especially brilliant in winter when the branches are bare and heavy with hips, and may be planted to give splashes of orange-red in any corner of the garden. It is most valuable, however, when, with careful annual pruning, it is grown over pergolas, *berceaux* and hedges.

Professor Gianfrancesco Fineschi, who has the most comprehensive collection of the genus *Rosa*, has kindly allowed me to draw on his knowledge for these notes.

Lady Hillingdon

'Lady Hillingdon' (1910).

Any Tea Rose bred and able to prosper in the open in England must be hardy; and if 1910 was, deservedly, the year of 'Rayon d'Or' (a golden-yellow remontant, then a complete novelty), there was more than honourable mention for 'Lady Hillingdon,' raised by the Lowe and Shawyer nurseries at Uxbridge. This was a vigorous Tea Rose with long, elegant buds developing slowly into scented ocher and corn-yellow flowers, their petals edged in creamy white.

It was dedicated to Lady Hillingdon, of Hillingdon Court near Uxbridge, whose husband came from a family distinguished in the world of politics, in finance and the Army. Both Uxbridge and Hillingdon have now been virtually absorbed into the metropolis, in the westward expansion of London.

The climbing variety of this rose, available from 1917 and prized for its colour, scent and the graceful curve of the stems, is still much appreciated for its tenacity and hardiness, as well as for a flowering which continues until the earliest frosts.

My thanks are due to Lady Bridges, British Ambassadress in Italy and a connoisseur of roses, for information on Lord and Lady Hillingdon.

Albertine

'Albertine' (1921).

The species from which this rose descends, the Japanese *Rosa wichuraiana*, a rambler with long, trailing shoots was until 1886 thought to be a variety of *Rosa luciae*, from which it differs in a few minor ways. *Rosa luciae* is, for instance, more widely distributed in the country of common origin, has longer leaflets (the terminal leaflet measuring about 5cm), and the flowers are smaller (about 2cm across). The name *wichuraiana* has, however, prevailed – the more easily because *Rosa luciae* seems never to have been introduced in Europe.

Descendants of these related roses have surprisingly divergent leaf- and flower-forms and flowering seasons, and may be either perfumed or scentless. Thus 'Albertine' and 'Albéric Barbier' are akin, 'Albertine' bearing the same relation to 'Dorothy Perkins' (itself a variety of *R. wichuraiana*) as that of 'Albéric Barbier' to the 'Dorothy Perkins' twin, 'Excelsa'; yet both have broad, early, scented flowers, whereas 'Dorothy Perkins' and 'Excelsa' are late-flowering, with small, scentless blooms.

'Albertine' is named after the eponymous character in Marcel Proust's *A l'ombre des jeunes filles en fleurs*, published in 1919. The coppery-pink colour of its slightly ruffled scented petals was very aptly described by Vita Sackville-West as "a beautiful soft pink that appears to have been dipped in tea."

Rosa laevigata 'Cooperi'

Rosa laevigata 'Cooperi' (introduced into Europe, 1921); syn. *Rosa cooperi*.

This rose has been known in Europe for 65 years by different names, and some botanists do not agree with the two used above. To the first it is objected that the plant may not be a variety of *R. laevigata* but an inter-specific, or "between-species" hybrid of *R. gigantea* and *R. laevigata*, the result of a chance crossing due to pollen from the latter carried by insects or the wind. The second name, *R. cooperi* includes no indication of botanic species; and many people favour the designation *R. gigantea*, var. 'Cooperi.'

Roland Cooper himself is, however, undisputable – the man who, newly appointed as Superintendent of the Maymyo Botanical Gardens in the Shan Hills of Burma, despatched seeds of the unknown rose to Ireland in 1921. The problems of identity aside, it proves a vigorous climber, glossy-leaved (occasionally showing the three leaflets of *R. laevigata*), with wide five-petalled flowers, white and scented. The single flowering season, long as it is, and a dislike of protracted frosty weather, are minor flaws in a rose which does so well in the right conditions.

Penelope

'Penelope' (1924).

Rose hips are most important to the English rose lover who after assessing the plant for desirable qualities, such as vigour of growth and flowering, scent, remontancy and resistance to disease, wants to know how plentiful the decorative "fruits" are going to be. (The true fruits, or achenes, usually thought to be seeds, lie within the receptacle.) 'Penelope,' having fulfilled the customary requirements, brilliantly passes the final test with a generous crop, though the hips are not of conventional red. They resemble bunches of big pink sugared almonds tinged, as they slowly ripen, with white and pale green.

The glory of a rose bush is, of course, the rose itself, and this one produces an initial, abundant and extensive flowering, after which the dead heads make room for a second burst of blossom. But the corollas of the later, lesser flowering may be left to wither where they are, to ensure such a decorative bonus.

'Penelope,' as a shrub rose with clusters of semi-double, quite small perfumed flowers is ideal for making a free-growing hedge. The breeder, the Revd Joseph Pemberton, a retired Anglican clergyman, was an impassioned and expert rosarian who wrote an invaluable book on his subject and had a special interest in hybridizing *Rosa moschata*. More about him will be found in our notes on the roses 'Mozart' and 'Buff Beauty.'

Dainty Bess

'Dainty Bess' (1925).

This is a scented rose with five broad petals and a central cluster of unexpectedly vivid red stamens. The lady whose name it bears had captivated the breeder, W.E.B. Archer, who not only offered her his loveliest flower but, as in a fairy-tale, asked her to marry him as well.

'Dainty Bess,' as the product of a cross between two Hybrid Teas, should, despite its five-petalled flowers and often multiple stems, be classed with the Hybrid Teas (as are many modern varieties which even at their first flowering carry several blooms on a stem). There was at the time a certain amount of prejudice against five-petalled hybrids and Archer, a devoted amateur turned professional rose breeder, set out to overcome it. From 1920 to 1940 his firm – to be known as W.E.B. Archer & Daughter – concentrated on the hybridization and distribution at Sellindge in Kent, producing several fine varieties besides 'Dainty Bess.' In 1927 his 'Daily Mail Scented Rose' won both the cup offered by that newspaper and the Gold Medal of the National Rose Society, and in the 1936 'Single-Flowered Hybrid Tea' class it was the turn of 'Ellen Willmott,' named for the distinguished author of *The Genus Rosa*. 'Dainty Bess,' entered in two competitions in 1925, before being introduced commercially, won the Gold Medal at the NRS's summer show for cut flowers and the Royal Horticultural Society's Award of Merit after test-growing in the trial grounds at Wisley in Surrey. The rose went on the market in the autumn of 1926 and it is the only one which, after 60 years and among the 2,500 varieties cultivated by the members of the American Rose Society, earns that Society's rating of 8.4/10.

Lady Sylvia

'Lady Sylvia' (1926).

The Russian professor S.G. Saakov, researching into the way in which certain roses will habitually produce sports, or mutants, finds the tendency very marked in the variety 'Ophelia.' He also notes that it is shared by varieties of mutant origin.

Mutants retaining the altered characteristics and appearance after a suitable trial period are said to be "fixed" and give rise to new varieties from which plants can in turn be propagated. The most frequently observed modifications are: a change from bushy to climbing habit; a partial or total change of colour in the petals; and a change to repeat-flowering from the single flowering of the parent.

The three successive mutations linking 'Ophelia' and the climbing variety of 'Lady Sylvia' are as follows:

'Ophelia' (1912)
↓
'Mme Butterfly' (1918)
↓
'Lady Sylvia' (1926)
↓
'Cl. Lady Sylvia' (1933)

'Ophelia,' 'Mme Butterfly' and 'Lady Sylvia' have long been popular as florists' roses for their elegance of form and soft pink colouring – deeper in 'Mme Butterfly,' deeper still in 'Lady Sylvia.' The latter has been called the most attractive Hybrid Tea of the late 1920s and early 1930s.

Rose des Maures

'Rose des Maures'; syn. 'Sissinghurst Castle.'

In 1930 Sir Harold Nicolson and his wife Vita Sackville-West – writer, poet, biographer and discriminating gardener – bought the castle of Sissinghurst in Kent and its surrounding land. The utterly neglected state of buildings and garden gave the new owners ample scope to exercise their particular gifts, she as an experienced and unconventionally minded gardener, he as director of the layout with an unusually keen eye for practical possibilities. And on an early summer morning of that same year, 1930, (as we read in the National Trust's booklet on Sissinghurst) Vita Sackville-West discovered, among the brambles in what had been an orchard bounded by a wide ditch, a long-lost variety of the ancient *Rosa gallica* – or *Rosa rubra*, as it was known before Linnaeus introduced the modern name.

'Rose des Maures' is a vigorous shrub, spreading, in a way typical of the ancestral *gallica*, by means of suckers and reaching a meter in height. The trailing branches are practically thornless, the late-spring flowers scented and violet-red.

The name 'Sissinghurst Castle' needs no explanation, but 'Rose des Maures' is a puzzle; unless it is, perhaps, a kind of literary reminiscence of the traditional fancy that roses of dark, uncommon hue must hail from northern Africa.

Betty Prior

'Betty Prior' (1932).

In the 1920s the Danish hybridizer Svend Poulsen created an important new breed of roses from a cross between the pink Polyantha 'Orléans Rose' and the semi-double Hybrid Tea 'Red Star.' The results of this happy union, 'Else Poulsen' and 'Kirsten Poulsen,' had the Polyantha attributes of continuous flowering and resistance to frost. Moreover, they were erect and tall, in contrast to their predecessors the Dwarf Polyanthas and they had larger flowers. The strain of Hybrid Polyanthas was born.

Svend Poulsen's father had attempted a similar cross ten years before, but his best seedling, 'Rodhatte' ('Red Riding Hood'), was for long infertile – as to a lesser degree were 'Else Poulsen' and 'Kirsten Poulsen' – and had few descendants. English breeders quickly realized the value of the new roses and the Colchester firm of Donald Prior and Sons, using pollen from 'Else Poulsen,' raised the variety 'Betty Prior,' which won a First Class Trial Ground Award from the National Rose Society in 1932. The Society's *Annual* for 1933 speaks of this rose as "very similar to 'Else Poulsen' but more floriferous than that variety and does not spot with rain." (A full-page colour photograph shows it in full flower on 6th November, 1932.) During the present decade its rating in the American Rose Society's *Handbook for Selecting Roses* has averaged 8.5/10.

AmTrechslin.

Signora Piero Puricelli

'Signora Piero Puricelli' (1935); syn. 'Signora.'

It was in the mid 1930s, as competition for the production of new roses grew ever keener, that Italy entered the lists. Germany had breeders like Lambert, Kordes and Tantau; Luxembourg had Ketten, Lens was working in Belgium, Poulsen in Denmark, and Buisman, de Ruiter, Leender and Verschuren were active in Holland. In the United Kingdom there were Cant, Dickson and McGredy, and in France Guillot, Mallerin, Gaujard. There were others, too, all famous and experienced. Yet in the four years leading up to the war, Domenico Aicardi of Sanremo was exporting his new varieties into Europe and America. His 'Saturnia' won Gold Medals at the Concorso Internazionale in Rome and at Portland, Oregon; he bred 'Gloria di Roma,' 'Eterna Giovinezza' and – perhaps the most admired of all – 'Signora Piero Puricelli.' This rose, known simply as 'Signora' outside Italy, also won the Gold Medal at Portland in 1937.

"The very large flower," says a descriptive article in a contemporary Italian magazine, "is goblet-shaped, full and scented, in colour a magnificent blend of flame-red, orange and salmon. A most vigorous rose, with strong, straight stems, growing to 1 meter, or 1.20 meters, in height and flowering profusely throughout the season until the first frosts. Unsuitable for standards, but tolerant of cold weather in this country."

Piero Puricelli was a well known civil engineer, president of a large construction company building roads in Europe and Africa before the last war. In compliment to him the new rose was dedicated to his wife, though the use by a married woman of her husband's Christian name is not customary in Italy; perhaps, in this case, it was thought more acceptable for the English- and French-speaking markets.

The variety 'Anne Marie Trechslin' introduced by Meilland in 1968, has many of the attributes which made 'Signora' a success, especially its form, scent and blended colouring.

Mozart

'Mozart' (1937).

The Church of England at the turn of the century produced not a few great and enthusiastic rosarians – men such as Dean S. Reynolds Hole and the Suffolk rector A. Foster-Melliar. Eminent among them was the Revd Joseph Pemberton, President of the National Rose Society in 1911–12, and originator of the Hybrid Musks.

His gardener J.A. Bentall, who ran the nursery after Pemberton's death, bred a rose named 'Ballerina,' which is known as the twin of 'Mozart.' And twins the two might be, for they were introduced in the same year and are similar in growth and appearance, as in the colour of their thickly clustered flowers. Yet Bentall raised one at Romford in Essex, Peter Lambert the other at Trier in Germany. The extraordinary resemblance is, perhaps, due to a common descent from 'Robin Hood' (itself descended from *R. moschata*), and both roses are regarded as perfect examples of hardy, vigorous Polyanthas. They are remontant, and flower quite profusely with thick clusters of small, brightly coloured blooms, almost always white-centered.

Buff Beauty

'Buff Beauty' (1939?).

This is a rose classified as a Hybrid Musk, though many writers consider the description inaccurate, given the somewhat remote connection with the species *Rosa moschata*. The family tree includes varieties of *Rosa chinensis*, of *Rosa multiflora*, and of the Hybrid Teas, and affinities between them all – often interesting and surprising – are accounted for by the presence of *Rosa moschata* as a common, distant ancestor.

This ancestor, the Wild Musk Rose whose origins lie, uncertainly, in southern Europe, North Africa and India, possessed two specific qualities: it flowered from late summer into autumn, and bore its scent not in the petals, but in the stamens and anthers. As the name implies, the fragrance resembled that of musk which, produced as a glandular secretion by the Asian hornless or Indian roe deer, *Moschus moschiferus*, is used in the scent industry as a concentrate and fixative.

The Hybrid Musks were first introduced by Joseph Pemberton (1852–1926). To begin with, he called them Hybrid Teas, but their scent and pale colours, the charmingly loose shape of the flowers and the shrubby but not rigid habit of growth confirmed his roses as an almost separate breeding group. They are represented today by 'Penelope' (1924), 'Cornelia' (1925), 'Felicia' (1928) and 'Buff Beauty,' apparently introduced in about 1939 and named from its apricot-yellow colour, not unlike that of fine natural leather.

Pemberton's sister Felicia, helped by his gardener J.A. Bentall, continued his work of hybridization and marketing after his death, until her own death three years later, when Bentall set up independently. The rose 'Buff Beauty,' however, has no properly attested history. Its origin, parentage, and even the date of its first going on sale, are unrecorded.

As far as the development of Hybrid Musks is concerned, the mantle of Pemberton seems to have descended on the Belgian breeder Louis Lens. From Pemberton's 'Robin Hood,' a variety he acquired in 1927, Lens had by 1984 produced a remarkable series of shrub roses named after composers – Puccini, Schubert, Sibelius, Verdi, Vivaldi – and bearing great quantities of small flowers.

Queen Elizabeth

'Queen Elizabeth' (1954).

This variety aroused enormous interest from the first: its habit, and the multiple flowered stems, were those of a Floribunda, but a Floribunda whose stems and inflorescence alike are as though seen through a magnifying glass. The Americans, reluctant to include it in the existing category, invented the entirely new one of Grandiflora for 'Queen Elizabeth.' The term, however, though widely accepted in the United States, is little used in Europe, where the American Grandifloras are classed as Floribundas.

This American rose was launched on a fortunate career when the Queen Elizabeth II, soon after her accession, granted it her name. By 1955 it had triumphed in the All-America Rose Selection won the American Rose Society's Gold Medal and the President's International Trophy of the Royal National Rose Society, and earned the title of "world's favourite." Many other European awards followed.

In three to four years it will grow head-high. It may be planted singly or, being remontant, tidy and profusely flowering, will make a fine hedge. It is also an elegant cut flower, with a light, pleasant scent.

'Queen Elizabeth' has justifiably been called ever reliable. In the American Rose Society's grading for 1986 it led the Grandifloras with the very high mark of 9.1/10.

Golden Wings

'Golden Wings' (1956).

This rose, its wide wing-shaped golden petals 12cm across, brought with it to Europe the glory of the American Rose Society's Gold Certificate, and in 1965 won the coveted Award of Merit from the Royal Horticultural Society in further recognition of the qualities developed during ten years of stringent trials in the United States.

Being fortunate enough to obtain one of the first specimens on sale in Italy, I set it in the corner of my garden reserved for favourite roses. A gardener's happiness is to be among his plants, and is increased when others also enjoy them. I remember a visit from a certain lady – a great flower lover, as she assured me – who asked to see the garden. I was, of course, delighted to take her round. Arriving in due course before 'Golden Wings' in full bloom I paused, waiting to hear her reaction "Well," she said "I never thought you'd also have wild roses here!" Clearly, to this great flower lover, any five-petalled rose was "wild." I hastily moved on to a bush of 'Super Star,' by then a very popular rose, its huge double flowers glowing orange-vermilion on their long stalks, and she was gratifyingly enthusiastic.

'Golden Wings' is a shrub rose, reaching head height and flowering from May to November and resistant to frost, though less so to hot and dry conditions. For the "Proof of the Pudding" award in America, given after extensive trials conducted in their own gardens by members of the American Rose Society, it gained almost 90% of the votes, and in 1972 was first in the Royal National Rose Society's place-list of remontant shrub roses. Roy E. Shepherd, who bred it, is an expert rosarian. His history of the rose, published in 1954, is still of value, and his garden at Medina, Ohio, contains an almost complete collection of existing botanical species, together with many other roses, old and new.

Mrs Jones

'Mrs Jones' (1958); syn. 'Centenaire de Lourdes.'

This rose, 'Centenaire de Lourdes' in France, was named in centenary celebration of the continuous series of miracles which has strengthened belief and shaken scepticism ever since the child Bernadette Soubirous had her vision of the Virgin Mary in the grotto at Lourdes in February, 1858. As though striving to live up to the miraculous overtones of its name, it is naturally graceful, vigorous and resistant to disease, while the semi-double flowers of luminous pink are produced over many months.

This was the first important variety obtained by André Chabert at the great French nurseries of Georges Delbard. After nearly 30 years it remains one of the most admired of the Cluster-Flowered roses, to use the Royal National Rose Society's term for the former Floribundas.

Pascali

'Pascali' (1963).

In 1873 Louis Lens, grandfather and namesake of the present owner of the famous Belgian firm, bought 12 hectares of land at Wavre-Nôtre-Dame, near Malines. Today most of the Lens roses are grown in the nursery he founded there.

The firm concentrated on new varieties from the 1920s onwards ('Ville de Malines' was one of the first, followed by 'Mme Louis Lens') and on a series of mutants from such established roses as 'Golden Sam McGredy,' 'Golden Vandal,' 'Golden Van Rossem,' and the climbing varieties of 'Roselandia,' 'Gloria Mundi' and 'Mme Louis Lens.' In 1956 Louis Lens inherited entire responsibility for the business, and its roses were in the hands, and close to the heart, of an expert, scholarly and dedicated rose lover whose achievements speak for themselves.

He has created many beautiful roses: a class of "mini-Floribundas," midway between the miniatures and the cluster-flowered shrub roses; shrub roses of a new kind, each with special characteristics: the early-flowering 'Springtime,' for example, or 'Pleine de Grace,' its long branches flower-laden from end to end; varieties of *Rosa moschata* named for the great composers ('Puccini,' 'Schubert,' 'Verdi' and so on); and, finally, the prostrate ground-cover roses, such as 'White Spray' and 'Tapis volant,' which answer the modern needs of the large garden where labour-saving is all-important.

The Hybrid Tea 'Pascali,' however, is the apple of his eye. He himself calls it the loveliest and most frequently rewarded white rose in the world, so it is, perhaps, superfluous to add the independent testimony of Ena Harkness, writing in the RNRS *Annual* after a referendum in 1972: "A really pure white rose is hard to find. 'Pascali' I find exquisite. Shapely and well filled with petals, this rose lasts longer in water than any white I know."

Papa Meilland

'Papa Meilland' (1963).

So-called "black roses" have always fascinated people, possibly because of a subconscious desire to possess that inexistent marvel, the true black rose.

The first "black" rose was obtained 100 years ago by the "wizard of Lyons," Joseph Pernet-Ducher and its colour is described by the French writer Henry Fuchs, an accurate and meticulous observer, as "fiery crimson, with a velvety violet pile, almost black." The American breeder McFarland sees the flower as darker than red, shading to tones so deep as to verge on black.

Roses in the red-violet-purple and near-black range are always strongly scented, and the fragrance is conditioned by climate. Some of the crimson roses of earlier decades – 'Étoile de Hollande,' 'Crimson Glory,' 'Josephine Bruce,' 'Charles Mallerin' or 'Chrysler Imperial' – predecessors of the deep red 'Papa Meilland,' are remembered as generally excellent; others, more vividly, for specific faults or virtues. 'Papa Meilland' itself has fine flowers and penetrating scent, but is not free-flowering and needs sunshine and warmth to do really well.

It is named after Antoine, founder of the Meilland nurseries, father of Francis, who did so much for the firm, and grandfather of Alain, the present owner.

Louksor

'Louksor' (originally 'Louqsor') (1966).

In his impressive autobiography, *Jardinier du Monde*, Georges Delbard pays generous tribute to his colleagues and assistants who, with their ready enthusiasm, deserve no small part of the credit for his success as a rose breeder.

His firm had at first specialized in fruit trees, with expert staff to raise them. By the mid 1950s, however, his knowledge of the market and his innate flair made Delbard develop the rose growing side of the business, for which task he sought the help of Jacques Chabert, an amateur breeder whose passion for roses had been nourished by Charles Mallerin, adviser for the last 20 years of his life to the young Francis Meilland. A meeting between Delbard and Chabert proved decisive. Before it was over Georges Delbard had arranged for Jacques, and his son André Chabert, to take over a section of the nurseries. When Jacques died a few months later, the young André found himself welcomed into the firm with his small collection of as yet unregistered roses and all Delbard's resources of nursery space, frames and greenhouses at his disposal for the work of hybridization and selection.

'Louksor' was produced from the pollen of a rose André brought with him, 'Dr Albert Schweitzer.' It is a reliable rose, though not showy, and a very attractive one. The 30 scented petals of a delicate apricot colour, suffused with yellow and pink and shading to luminous gold at the base, make it a charming cut flower. There are not many roses, like this, *qui font les beaux bouquets*, and not many which remain popular for so long; 'Louksor' has been a main attraction in Delbard's catalogue for 20 years.

Baronne Edmond de Rothschild

'Baronne Edmond de Rothschild' (1967).

On 23rd June, 1967 the Geneva International Rose Trials celebrated their 20th anniversary with a programme of events ranging from talks attended by a knowledgeable audience drawn from many countries to a concluding reception in the grounds of Baron Edmond de Rothschild's fairy-tale lakeside château de Prégny. His young wife, Nadine, welcomed the guests and, with the Alps towering in the background, a dialogue from *Le Petit Prince* by Antoine de Saint-Exupéry was performed, followed by extracts from Rilke, Shakespeare, Brecht and Ronsard, all on the subject of roses.

After the entertainment Mme Louisette Meilland presented the hostess with a magnificent bouquet of the powerfully scented pink and silver roses, which were at once named after her to mark the occasion. Anne Marie Trechslin, who was also a guest, added the gift of her watercolour of the new, and appropriately named, rose.

A.M.Trechslin.

Anne Marie Trechslin

'Anne Marie Trechslin' (1968).

Rose breeders may dedicate their roses to important or well known people, to relations or to friends (though never, by an unwritten rule, to themselves), and two good reasons exist for the naming of 'Anne Marie Trechslin.' The dedication pays tribute not only to the skill of one of the world's foremost rose painters, but to all her efforts in spreading knowledge of the flowers, and a consequent demand for them.

Two hundred and twenty watercolours, illustrating four books, make up a body of work to rank close to the three celebrated volumes of Pierre Joseph Redouté's *Les Roses*, a century and a half earlier. Anne Marie Trechslin is a sensitive and versatile artist, who catches the ephemeral beauty of a rose while respecting every botanical detail. The powerfully scented variety named after her, illustrated here with the subtle shading of its many tints, is a perfect reflection of her style.

Just Joey

'Just Joey' (1972).

When this rose gained a Trial Ground Certificate from the Royal National Rose Society in 1971 it was described as having full flowers, borne singly or several to a stem, with 32 petals of coppery orange, red-veined and paling towards the edges. Growth: tall and upright. Foliage: matt, dark green, small, reddish when young.

The RNRS's system of judging differs from systems used elsewhere in Europe, both in the composition of the jury – which consists of exclusively British experts – and in the allocation of points out of 100. Roses from the Trial Ground at St Albans in Hertfordshire may receive 20 for vigour and habit (of growth), 20 for resistance to disease, and 20 for the flower or inflorescence and its colour. Abundance of flowering, repeat-flowering, novelty and overall effect take 30 points between them, and there are ten points for scent.

"Oh, just Joey," said Roger Pawsey when asked what he would call the rose he had bred at the long-established firm of Cant at Colchester in Essex, of which he was director. His wife's name was Josephine.

In 1978 the Royal National Rose Society voted 'Just Joey' third of the year's top 12 Hybrid Teas, one point behind 'Alec's Red' and 'Silver Jubilee,' which tied for first place. It then won the prize for best scented variety at the International Concours at The Hague, an award which according to the other British growers surprised nobody except Roger Pawsey himself. In 1986, as the public's favourite rose, 'Just Joey' was awarded the beautiful, handsomely wrought James Mason Gold Medal.

New Daily Mail

'New Daily Mail' (1972); syn. 'Puszta.'

We are all too often apt to establish rose categories of varying validity and usefulness, and to concentrate on the winner. The world's favourite, the most highly perfumed, the reddest of the red or longest-lasting as a cut flower, takes the lead. A tactful silence reigns over the runners-up.

Nevertheless, let us here consider an honest second-place rose, bred by Mathias Tantau, whose nurseries are regarded by some as the top, and by others as the second-best, in Germany. It is a vigorous, shrubby rose, scarcely suggesting the Hungarian steppe of its original name. The clusters of symmetrical semi-double flowers are wide and erect, of a deep, glowing crimson which neither fades nor parches. It has been dismissed as "the usual red, cluster-flowering rose," yet it gained the coveted award of the *Anerkannte Deutsche Rose*. Altogether, we may accord it a good second place.

The hybridizer and propagator, Mathias Tantau, is head of the great firm inherited from his father at Uetersen, near Hamburg, little more than 30 kilometers from the other celebrated establishment, that of Kordes, where the rose known as 'Korresia' in Great Britain ('Friesia' in Germany) was produced in 1973. With 'Super Star,' 'Fragrant Cloud' and 'Blue Moon' – to mention only three of his foremost varieties – Tantau has added to the beauty of gardens all over the world: it is not so easy, then, to assess his proper place.

Korresia

'Korresia' (1973); syn. 'Sunsprite' (in America), 'Friesia' (in Germany).

Kordes, the biggest breeders in central Europe, named this rose, originally, after their own part of Holstein, Northern Germany. In Friesia they have hybridized, selected and cultivated all their roses, first at Elmshorn and since 1910 at Sparrieshoop, where a third generation of the family is at the helm. Wilhelm Kordes, who founded the firm in 1887, was succeeded by his son Wilhelm, regarded as the greatest rose man of all time. In 1964 this Wilhelm handed over the whole concern to his own son, Reimer, who had worked with him for years and is a worthy inheritor.

As examples we may quote a few of the famous roses raised by Wilhelm Kordes II in his 50 years of active, scientific hybridization: 'Crimson Glory' (1935), 'Orange Triumph' (1937), 'Frühlingsgold' (1937), 'Frühlingsmorgen' (1940) and 'Kordes Sondermeldung' (1940); to say nothing of the descendants of the species *Rosa kordesii*, seed parent of repeat-flowering and frost-resistant ramblers.

During his long apprenticeship under his father Reimer Kordes had already produced such highly successful varieties as 'Lilli Marlene,' 'Königin der Rosen,' 'Isabel de Ortiz' and 'Wiener Charm.' As director he has proved his gifts again with florists' roses such as 'Prominent' and 'Mercedes' for example, as well as roses for bedding. The latter include 'Iceberg,' 'Peer Gynt' and 'Korresia,' a lovely scented Floribunda which when launched commercially won the most important prize in Germany, the *Anerkannte Deutsche Rose*, and was nominated first among the yellow Floribundas.

Sweet Promise

'Sweet Promise' (1973); syn. 'Sonia,' 'Sonia Meilland.'

Sonia Meilland is the granddaughter of Francis and Louisette Meilland, of the famous family of rosarians which Antoine Meilland founded. Her rose, the attractive pale pink buds touched with yellow and salmon tones, is a florists' favourite and the most widely sold of its colour range in the world.

Florists' roses are normally excluded from this book, for special hybridization procedures are employed in breeding them, the selection cycle differs from that of garden roses, and they are cultivated under glass, with careful control of light, temperature and humidity to determine both the quality and the quantity of the results. Nowadays, on the other hand, leading growers test and select all their garden roses in the open, even when the plants are destined for other countries and climatic conditions.

But 'Sweet Promise,' a star among greenhouse roses, is here as a shining exception, since it enjoys equal success out of doors, either for cut flowers or for bedding. In the United States it is known as a Grandiflora, that almost entirely North American class of large and vigorous roses with several wide-spreading flowers to a stem.

Yesterday

'Yesterday' (1974).

The Polyantha roses popular at the end of the nineteenth century may have derived from crossing between a variety of *Rosa chinensis* known as 'Minima' and the first European seedlings of the Oriental *Rosa multiflora*. The new strain, low-growing and in flower from spring to autumn, brought into the garden a longer spell of colour than was conceivable before its introduction. Pollinated by Hybrid Teas, these Dwarf Polyanthas produced the Hybrid Polyanthas; and from them, in turn, were bred the Floribundas whose flowers, though still in clusters, were more like those of the Hybrid Teas. In a few years, apparently, a fresh group had been created.

'Yesterday' is linked, as its name implies, to the older roses, but what it seems to herald, in vigour, in generous and successive flowering and in the form of the narrow scented petals, is a Polyantha revival. Such a revival, going back to 'Ballerina' and 'Mozart' in 1937, continues in England with 'Marjorie Fair' (bred, as was 'Yesterday' itself, by Jack Harkness), and 'Sally Holmes' from the breeder R.A. Holmes. From the Lens nurseries in Belgium comes a rose called 'Rush.' These, and many other excellent modern shrubs, promise a new era for the Polyanthas.

Nil Bleu

'Nil Bleu' (1976).

Blue flowers being as rare as they are, gardeners are apt to take considerable liberties with the dictionary definition of that colour. What they happily call blue roses might well be better described at times as lavender, mauve, lilac-pink or violet. Perhaps, in naming 'Nil Bleu,' Delbard and Chabert (the distributor and hybridizer respectively) were hoping to assist an overworked adjective.

The best "blue" rose since 1964 has been the strongly scented 'Blue Moon' (known in Germany as 'Mainzer Fastnacht,' and as 'Sissi' in France), which is actually bluish pink. 'Nil Bleu' drew level with this competitor by winning 12 international awards within months of its introduction in France, four of them as best scented variety. Moreover, it has the wider petals – they can be nearly 20 centimeters across – and the flowers when cut retain their heady perfume for several days longer than do those of 'Blue Moon.'

Julie Delbard

'Julie Delbard' (1976).

Georges Delbard named this variety after his first granddaughter. The flowers, he said, reminded him of butterflies with out-stretched wings – an exact and poetic image for the delicate corollas with their broad, wavy petals. They change in the light from salmon-pink to pale apricot and melt to flesh-tones, the shifting colours illuminated by a glowing yellow at the base of the petals.

'Julie Delbard,' as its ancestry shows, was deliberately bred to give colour. All the many preliminary crossings are between famous garden roses of recent years, five of them ('Zambra,' 'Orange Triumph,' 'Floradora,' 'Orléans Rose' and 'Goldilocks') being cluster-flowered, and two ('Bettina' and 'Rouge Mallerin') having one flower to a stalk.

It is thus a rose to ornament any garden, and the great splashes of colour won it a Gold Medal at the international event held in the Parque del Oeste at Madrid. But it is also a rose for indoors, better displayed against the light walls of modern rooms than in a heavier, more traditional setting, and lending its airy grace to imaginative flower arrangements.

Grand Siècle

'Grand Siècle' (1976).

The *Grand Siècle*, that century of grand-scale conquest and achievement during which Louis XIV, God's representative on earth, arbiter and architect of every enterprise, ruled for over 50 years in France, has always fascinated Georges Delbard. This rose, in his opinion, is fittingly named because of its grandeur; it is "the stateliest of pink roses." And, he adds, *"quel parfum suave!"*

Ten years before 'Grand Siècle' was launched Delbard had bred 'Versailles,' naming it after the palace that Louis built as witness to the luxury, and the high level of art and taste, of the age. Both these roses – the earlier, less opulent and almost scentless 'Versailles' and the magnificent, heavily scented 'Grand Siècle' – have won many international awards; they seem related in their colouring of pale sugar-pink shading to luminous, pearly white, as much as in the historical source of their names.

Double Delight

'Double Delight' (1976).

Some see the promised "double delight" of this rose resembling a luscious confection topped with whipped cream and streaked with cherry-juice, in its two handsomely contrasting colours. Others will think of the combination between its sculptured form and strong scent.

'Double Delight' performs differently under different regional conditions; tests confirm that it flowers better and more freely with plenty of strong sun than in places where it receives less sun and the light is feebler.

This unusual sensitivity to light, and the fact that it does not flower fully until the second year after transplanting, have influenced the American Rose Society's evaluation, which has gradually increased from 1/10 in 1977, when the rose was first considered, to 9/10 i.e. "outstanding," by 1986.

Margaret Merril

'Margaret Merril' (1978).

There are growers with a prejudice against white roses which, they believe, their customers dislike. And so some customers may, but not all. For over 150 years 'Mme Hardy' has been appreciated as the loveliest white rose ever seen, its fine lacework of petals crowding round the conical, emerald-green "eye"; and at the end of the nineteenth century came the Hybrid Perpetual 'Frau Karl Druschki,' or 'Snow Queen,' which for another 50 years took pride of place in florists' windows and in flowerbeds, despite the fact that its large blooms were scentless. The scented white rose was apparently a thing of the past until Charles Mallerin having made a bet to produce one within five years, duly succeeded with 'Neige Parfum' in 1940. This was followed by such famous white roses as 'Pascali,' 'Youki San,' and 'Iceberg,' each of them notable for some particular quality or qualities, and finally by 'Margaret Merril,' culmination of the series, whose flowers, though carried several to a stem, are large, elegant, and more fragrant than those of any other white rose. The three qualities of scent, colour and shape have won 'Margaret Merril' an enviable number of international prizes – three Gold and two Silver Medals, three Certificates of Merit, and four awards for the most highly scented variety.

Anne Harkness

'Anne Harkness' (1978).

This rose was raised by the remarkable Jack Harkness, and named in honour of a niece on her 21st birthday. It is notable for the graceful clusters of shapely, apricot-coloured blooms; for the long and sustained flowering which – as though 'Anne Harkness' were making a deliberately delayed entrance – begins two weeks after that of other Floribundas; and for its worldwide trade name, 'Harkaramel.'

Jack Harkness we have mentioned already. He is an outstanding rose breeder and a brilliant popularizer of roses. His biography, if he would only write it, would be full of anecdotes – stories of impulsiveness and impatience and devotion to his work, all told with feeling and spiked with wit. As it is, the dedication to his book *Roses* gives a taste of his style: "To Betty Catherine Harkness. I met her in 1946 and had the extraordinary sagacity to marry her in 1947, and we lived happily ever after, thanks mainly to her."

Paradise

'Paradise' (1979).

'Paradise' was included in the All-American Rose Selection in the very year of its introduction, a distinction it owed to the shape and unusual colour of its flowers, which are mauve-pink edged with ruby-red.

The oldest association of rose enthusiasts is the Royal National Rose Society of Great Britain, whose members numbered 100,000 at its centenary in 1976. In the United States the American Rose Society makes the prestigious All-American Rose Selection, which has included many of the roses illustrated in this book. Its procedure, briefly, is as follows. Breeders from America and elsewhere send their new roses to the various experimental stations of the Society in different parts of the United States, and the specimens are grown for two years in trial conditions under expert supervision. At the end of that time there is a scrutiny and up to four of the finalists are listed in the All-American Rose Selection. Such listing is a tremendous honour, valued even more highly in the United States than in other countries.

'Paradise' is a variety bred in California and distributed in Europe by Meilland. It does best in a situation where it can enjoy the morning sun and some shade in the afternoon.

Regensberg

'Regensberg' (1979); syn. 'Buffalo Bill.'

Sam McGredy, fourth of his name in direct line, was just two years old when his father died. Educated first in his native Ulster and subsequently in America and England, he came home at the age of 20 without the remotest idea of what skills were required to run the family business of rose breeding, or along what lines to do so. But tradition prevailed. He embarked on a serious course of study in rose genetics and the techniques of hybridization, and before assuming control of the firm he went abroad to learn his craft with both Gene S. Boerner, research director of Jackson and Perkins, the American (and self-styled "world's largest") rose growers, and Wilhelm Kordes in Germany. Kordes maintained that hybridization results depend 80% on the laws of genetics and less than 20% on chance. Therefore, he believed, only a minimum of the sowings made will point to any fresh development. He believed that garden roses were for providing masses of colour, not flower-shop specimens, and should be resistant to cold and disease. Above all, he believed in new ideas.

True to these principles, McGredy has not only bred roses of orthodox type but introduced a new strain of ground-cover Miniatures, as well as what he calls his "hand-painted" roses. Their flowers, in generous clusters, have red and white markings on the upper surface of the slightly flattened petals, the colours irregular in outline as waves on the shore. 'Picasso' was the first, in 1970, followed by 'Matangi' and 'Old Master' in 1974, 'Eye Paint' (1976), 'Priscilla Burton' (1978), 'Regensberg' (1979) – illustrated opposite, with low-growing, with wide open flowers – and 'Sue Lawley' (1980). The series continues, and we may be sure that more "hand-painted" or otherwise unusual roses are to come.

Saint Victor

'Saint Victor' (1979).

On a sunny summer day, 21st June, 1975, the *Société Française des Roses* bestowed on Saint-Victor-sur-Loire the coveted title of *Village des Roses*. Saint-Victor on its plateau is surrounded by woods and clearings, half hidden in trees, with an old castle of white stone, a medieval church and red-roofed houses. Five kilometers away, and five hectares in extent, is the rose garden instituted by Monsieur Jean Marc when he was Director of Parks and Gardens in the large industrial center of Saint-Etienne, close by. In 1970 the village became officially part of the town, which thus gained the enjoyment of wide, peaceful country views, a neighbouring lake, and the garden, where 30,000 rose bushes flower in succession from June to November.

In recognition of his work at Saint-Etienne and Saint-Victor, Jean Marc had a rose named after him by Paul Croix, his son-in-law. And it was Paul Croix, a noted breeder, who, by crossing 'Queen Elizabeth' with 'Mme Tsiranana' obtained the large, glowing scarlet rose which he called 'Saint Victor' – choosing that name, too, for its associations.

As for the saint, he was a Roman officer stationed at Marseilles early in the fourth century, when Maximian was Emperor of the West. He was also a devout Christian. When a visit from Maximian was announced, and the conventional gestures of Emperor-worship had to be made, the many Christians in the town were too terrified of the Imperial troops to listen to Victor's appeals for fortitude. Arrested while exhorting his co-religionists, he refused to abjure in spite of tortures and flogging, and was crushed to death under a millstone.

Robusta

'Robusta' (1979); syn. 'Kordes' Rose Robusta.'

In the 1980 edition of the stud-book *Modern Roses* 'Robusta' is shown as having for seed parent an unknown seedling and, as pollinator, *Rosa rugosa*, a very hardy species rose, famously resistant to mildew. The presence of *rugosa* in the pedigree bears out the breeding principles of Kordes, whose roses are invariably healthy and hardy, withstanding cold and little prone to disease.

The 1981 *Annual* of the Royal National Rose Society, however, prints this parentage in reverse (*i.e. Rosa rugosa* x seedling). The difference is more important than it may seem to non specialists, for there are breeders who believe the seed parent, or "mother" – always named first – to be responsible for certain given characteristics, while the pollen parent, or "father," transmits others. It is therefore essential to know which parent is which.

Certainly the anonymous seedling and its ancestors have contributed as much as *Rosa rugosa* to the quality-determining chromosomes of 'Robusta.' To *rugosa* we may attribute the vigour and bushiness implied in the very name, and the dark, shiny leathery leaves. More mysterious is the origin of the rapidity of growth in height and spread, the brilliant crimson of the concave, single blooms, and the uninterrupted spring-to-autumn flowering.

In 1980 this rose gained two major awards – a Certificate of Merit from the RNRS and, in Germany, the *Anerkannte Deutsche Rose*.

Laura

'Laura' (1981).

For some years now there have been new rules for the designation of varieties. The trade name (which is the same in every country) may no longer be either a proper name, such as 'Mme A. Meilland,' or a common noun, such as 'Yesterday.' It has to be a composite, consisting usually of the first two or three letters of the breeder's name and a sort of coded individual reference. '*Del*nil-ble,' for example, stands for Delbard's 'Nil Blue.' What is more, the names of varieties, hitherto permanent, can be changed from country to country to suit the sound or meaning of a language or, should the breeder so wish, be transferred from varieties at the end of their careers to others recently introduced. Thus the highly perfumed rose bred by Tantau and known as 'Duftwolke' in Germany is 'Fragrant Cloud' in the English-speaking world, *Nuage Parfumé* in France, *Nuvola Profumata* in Italy, and everywhere its trade name is *Tan*ellis. The name 'Cocktail,' which in the 1950s and 60s denoted a climber happy in a Mediterranean climate now belongs to a handsome yellow rose seen in florists' shops.

All this may help to explain why the 'Laura' illustrated opposite is not the 'Laura' to be found in catalogues of 20 years ago, but a vigorous grower with vivid, orange-red petals, brighter at the edges. It was bred by Meilland and marketed in the autumn of 1981.

Princesse de Monaco

'Princesse de Monaco' (1982).

Rose growers owe a great deal to the late Francis Meilland. As well as breeding the rose of the century, 'Peace,' he did much to ensure that the plant breeders of Europe had proper patents and received royalties. For a quarter of a century he propagated beautiful roses and distributed them all over the world. Thirty years ago he raised a rose named 'Grace de Monaco.'

Predictably, in the royal gardens at Monaco there was an enormous flowerbed containing 200 'Grace de Monaco' roses. But as time went by, some of them began to look past their best; and Alain Meilland, who, with his mother Louisette, had taken over the firm when his father died in 1958, was called in. Deciding to renew the whole bed, he found, to his amazement, that not a nursery in Europe could supply enough plants of what, just 25 years before, had been among the most popular roses grown.

Then the 1982 *Salon de la Rose* was held in the Principality, and Her Serene Highness performed the opening ceremony. She lingered at the exhibition, delighted with its high quality and obviously much attracted to one of Alain Meilland's new roses. The ivory-white petals, tinged with red at the edges caught her eye, for the colouring was that of the Monegasque flag. At once the breeder, breaking every rule of protocol, asked her permission to call the rose 'Grace de Monaco.' She granted the request, and within days 200 bushes were planted at the palace. The faded flowerbed was thus restored to its former glory.

Banzai '83

'Banzai '83' (1983).

The members of the Meilland Selection Committee are clearly fascinated by the Eastern promise in the name 'Banzai.' Mme Louisette Meilland – who married Francis in 1939 – raised the first 'Banzai' in 1960 from a cross between 'Radar' and 'Caprice.' The latter, a shrub rose of 1946, deserves to be better known. It had glossy dark leaves and large bicoloured flowers of strawberry-red and creamy white, the first to open in spring and last to fade in autumn. In 1976 the name was used again for a rose bred by Mme Meilland's father, Francesco Paolino; and finally came 'Banzai '83,' sold from the autumn of 1983 onwards in Denmark, Holland, Switzerland and Germany.

Being no philologist, though to a certain extent a dictionary-addict, I had always believed, until this rose appeared, that the word *banzai* was of Japanese origin. But then a good dictionary revealed that *ban* means "ten thousand" and *zai*, "years." The word is a greeting, a wish for long life to the person addressed, and, perhaps, the rose, too, is endowed with longevity, for it is sound and robust and easy to grow. The maize-tinted petals are edged irregularly in orange-red, shading off towards the center. The spherical flowers are semi-double and even when rained on the closely packed petals never stick together. It is almost as if they were separated by thin films of plastic.

The flowers are, sadly, unscented. But one expert, not entirely unconnected with the breeding of 'Banzai '83,' declares that, with perfume, this would be the most beautiful rose in the world.

Candy Rose

'Candy Rose' (1984).

This rose (whose name seems to suggest a likeness between its ten pink-and-white petals and the striped sugar-sweets so unfailingly popular on both sides of the Atlantic) is a vigorous grower, perfect for covering a slope or draping a wall. In late summer and autumn it carries a good crop of hips, though few flowers.

Increasingly, in recent years, roses have been bred for their cost- and labour-saving qualities as well as for their beauty. The aim has been to produce roses that demand little or no pruning save in winter, that resist lowest winter temperatures and the common fungus diseases, and will be, for these and other reasons, simple to look after. Such are the *Meidiland* or *Meillandécor* roses which, since they are not grafted, never throw up suckers. They include 'Candy Rose,' 'Ferdy' and 'Swany,' which are trailing and prostrate, and 'Bonica '82,' 'La Sevillana' and 'Pink Sevillana,' which may be planted singly, in groups, or to form hedges.

Besides adding to the number of freely flowering shrub roses available, many growers have concentrated on the ground-cover type. Thus the Japanese hybridist Susumu Onadera has 'Nozomi,' with its wealth of small, single, pearl-white blossom; and in 1980 Sam McGredy brought out a white Miniature, 'Snow Carpet.'

In 1964 'Sea Foam,' the first ground-cover rose to be marketed as such, was an exciting novelty. Today the choice is too large for more than a handful of its successors to be named here: 'Fairyland' (Harkness), 'Lavender Dream' (Interplant), 'Pink Spray' and 'White Spray' (Lens), 'Heidekönig' and 'Repandia' (Kordes), together with varieties from McGredy, Poulsen, Dickson and other famous hybridizers.

130

Pierre de Ronsard

'Pierre de Ronsard' (1986); syn. 'Eden Rose.'

For the French poet Pierre de Ronsard (1524–85) the rose often symbolized, or was associated with, love, and he wrote of it thus:

> *Mignonne, allons voir si la rose*
> *Qui ce matin avoit desclose*
> *Sa robe de pourpre au Soleil …*

When Ronsard was at the peak of his poetic career in the latter half of the sixteenth century, Dutch horticulturalists had succeeded in introducing the first varieties of *Rosa centifolia hollandica* – varieties enthusiastically welcomed by gardeners, and which would provide favourite subjects for artists of the Flemish school.

Despite their name, these roses were unrelated to the *Rosa centifolia* mentioned by Tertullian in *De Corona* and by the Greek philosopher Theophrastus in his writings on plants centuries earlier. (It is also found in Pliny the Elder, who follows Theophrastus implicitly.) Their origins were more probably haphazard. After all, no one knew anything about controlled pollination until the early 1800s.

Yet this 'Pierre de Ronsard' is interestingly close to the roses of the Flemish painters, though we need attribute the resemblance to no particular genetic factor; and those roses, with their classical namesake, have long disappeared.

Meillandina

'Meillandina' (1980–1986).

Miniature rose bushes, with their Lilliputian flowers and foliage, are said to derive from a *Rosa chinensis minima*, often heard of but never grown in the West. The first varieties were bred and distributed in France, where the climber 'Pompon de Paris' (perhaps identical with 'Rouletii,' discovered in 1922), was extremely popular from the early nineteenth century onwards and is the origin of many modern Miniatures. A hundred years ago, crossed with tea-scented roses, it gave rise to two varieties, 'Cécile Brunner' and 'Perle d'Or,' still admired for their elegance and perfume. Then interest in Miniatures waned until, in 1935 or so, it was revived by Jan de Vink in Holland and Pedro Dot in Spain. Since 1970 the tiny roses have had immense success in the United States, where Ralph Moore breeds them.

The Meillandinas, introduced in the 1980s, are a strain of small bushes with neat foliage, remontant and remarkably prolific. The double flowers are relatively wide and there is a wonderful range of colours – orange, lemon-yellow, apricot, pink, bright red, and white.

Hothouse grown miniature roses (in time, for instance, for St Valentine's Day) cannot be kept for very long in centrally heated rooms. The air is too dry for them and they have insufficient light. It is best to put the pot, usually containing two or three plants, on to a covered veranda and transfer it to the garden or balcony when warmer weather comes.

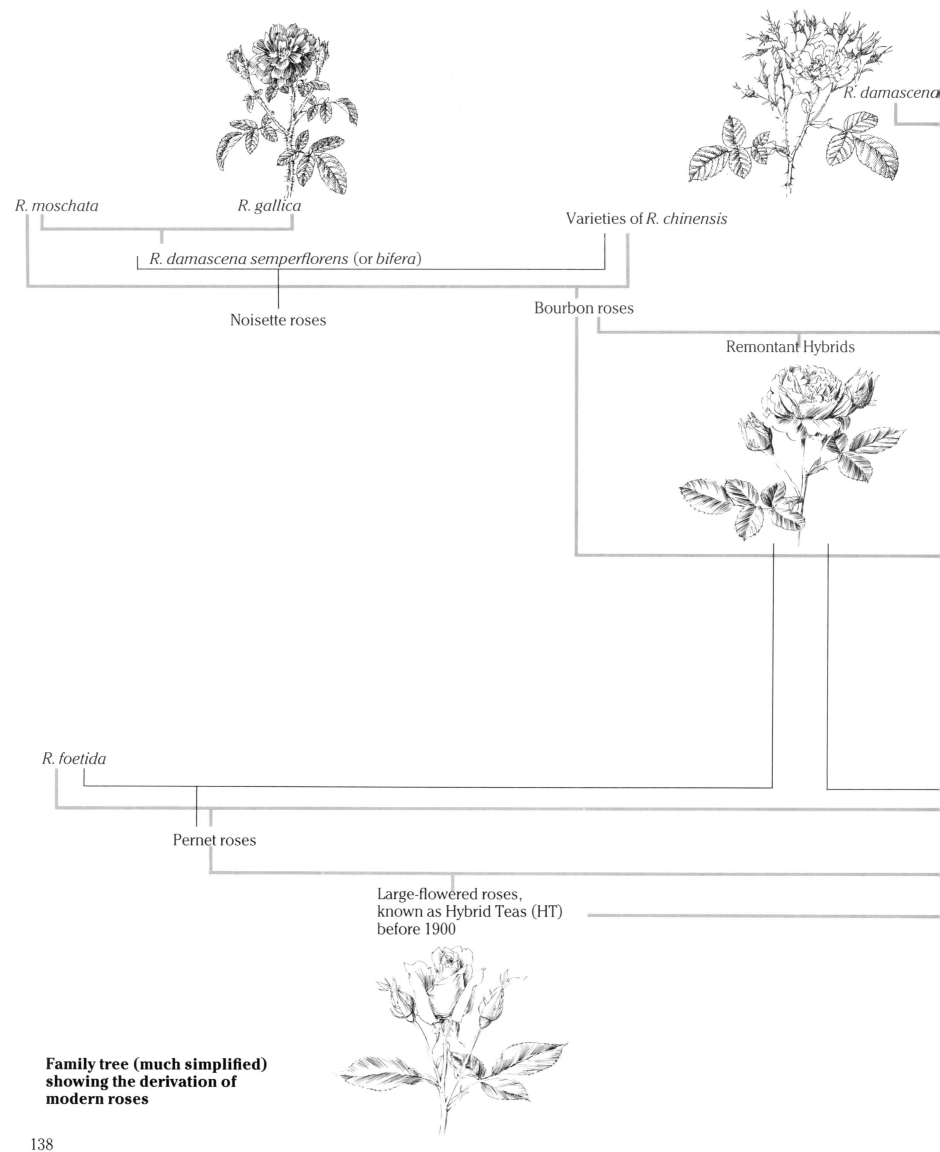

R. damascena

R. moschata

R. gallica

Varieties of R. chinensis

R. damascena semperflorens (or bifera)

Bourbon roses

Noisette roses

Remontant Hybrids

R. foetida

Pernet roses

Large-flowered roses,
known as Hybrid Teas (HT)
before 1900

**Family tree (much simplified)
showing the derivation of
modern roses**

138

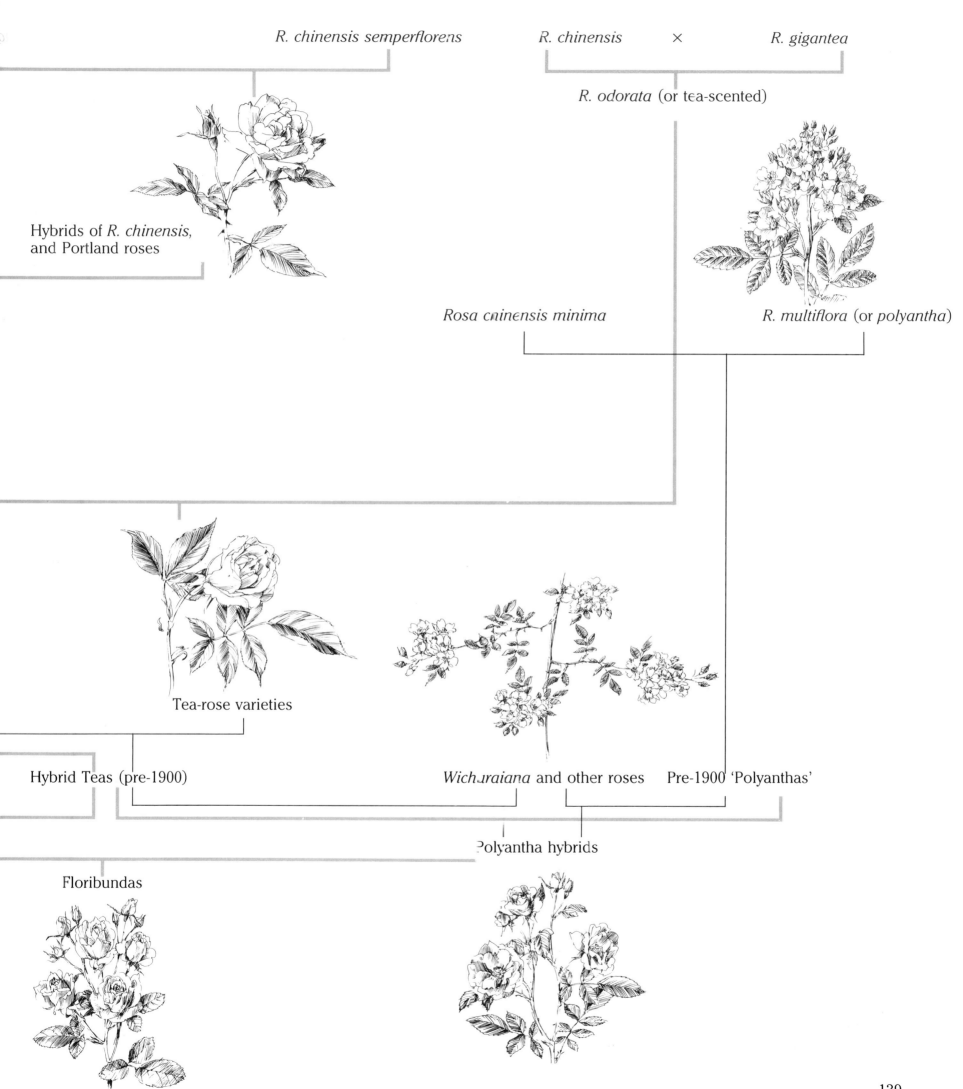

R. chinensis semperflorens

R. chinensis × R. gigantea

R. odorata (or tea-scented)

Hybrids of R. chinensis, and Portland roses

Rosa chinensis minima

R. multiflora (or polyantha)

Tea-rose varieties

Hybrid Teas (pre-1900)

Wichuraiana and other roses

Pre-1900 'Polyanthas'

Polyantha hybrids

Floribundas

Bibliography

Bean, W.J. *Trees and Shrubs Hardy in the British Isles*, London, 1970–80 (Eighth edition, four volumes)

Coggiatti, S. and Trechslin, A.M. *Roses d'antan*, Berne, 1975

Coggiatti, S. and Trechslin, A.M. *Rose antiche–Rose moderne*, Zurich, 1985

Gault, S.M. and Synge, P.M. *The Dictionary of Roses in Colour*, London, 1971

Harkness, J. *Roses*, London, 1978

Harkness, J. *The Makers of Heavenly Roses*, London, 1985

Krussmann, G. *Roses*, London, 1982

Modern Roses 8, American Rose Society, Harrisburg, 1980

Rose Annual, American Rose Society, Shreveport, 1955–85

Rose Annual, The Royal National Rose Society, London and St Albans, 1907–85

Shepherd, R.E. *History of the Rose*, New York, 1954

Simon, L. and Cochet, P. *Nomenclature de tous les noms de roses*, Paris, 1906

Singer, M. *Dictionnaire des roses*, two volumes, Brussels, 1885

Thomas, G.S. *Shrub Roses of Today*, London, 1974

Thomas, G.S. *Climbing Roses Old and New*, London, 1978

Thomas, G.S. *The Old Shrub Roses*, London, 1978

Willmott, E. *The Genus Rosa*, two volumes, London, 1910–14

Young, N. *The Complete Rosarian*, London, 1971

Index